My
Horse Riding
Journal

by

Angharad Thompson Rees

Published by

Little Whimsey Press

THIS HORSE RIDING JOURNAL
BELONGS TO

Sophia

keep your
hooves off!

Howdy, Horse Lover!

Here's how to use your journal!

Get a pen and pencil and start scribbling in your journal! All the best bits, the funny bits, and favourite moments shared with your four-legged friends - find a page and fill it in!

You'll find places to doodle and spaces for photos...

You'll discover quizzes to help improve your horsey-ness

Somewhere, scattered amongst the journal are colouring pages, a horsey story, and a pony poem - with spaces for you to create your own too! Awesome!

But most importantly of all, you'll find diary spaces to journal each riding session you have. Fill in the name of the horse you rode, age, colour, height, and what happened. Epic!

Are you up for the challenge to fill ALL the pages?!

Go on, have a go!

Name: Gwen

Height: 13 or 14

Age: ?

Colour: Paint - brown and white

What Happened Today : Gwen was wild and kicked a lot while she was cantering really really fast!

Stick a
A Pony Photo
HERE!

I ♥
Horses

Name: _____

Height: _____

Age: _____

Colour: _____

What Happened Today : _____

_____

_____

_____

_____

_____

_____

_____

_____

Draw a Doodle!

I ♥ Horses

Name: _____

Height: _____

Age: _____

Colour: _____

What Happened Today : _____

_____

_____

_____

_____

_____

_____

_____

_____

_____

Stick a
A Pony Photo
HERE!

I ♥ Horses

Can you Name 10 horse colours?

1 _____

2 _____

3 _____

4 _____

5 _____

6 _____

7 _____

8 _____

9 _____

10 _____

CAN YOU NAME ALL THE PARTS OF THE BRIDLE?

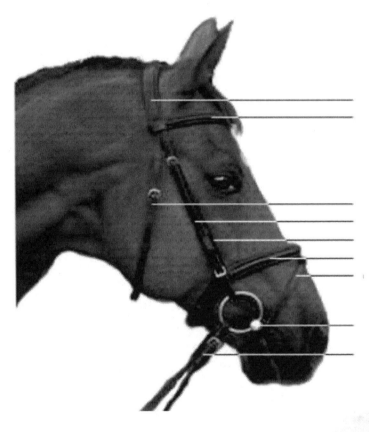

Name: _____

Height: _____

Age: _____

Colour: _____

What Happened Today : _____

_____

_____

_____

_____

_____

_____

_____

_____

_____

Draw a Doodle!

I ♥ Horses

Name: _____

Height: _____

Age: _____

Colour: _____

What Happened Today : _____

_____

_____

_____

_____

_____

_____

_____

_____

Stick a
A Pony Photo
HERE!

I ♥ Horses

Can you name 10 horse breeds?

1 _____

2 _____

3 _____

4 _____

5 _____

6 _____

7 _____

8 _____

9 _____

10 _____

Name: _____

Height: _____

Age: _____

Colour: _____

What Happened Today : _____

_____

_____

_____

_____

_____

_____

_____

_____

_____

Colour me In

My Top Ten Horse Books & Stories

1 _____

2 _____

3 _____

4 _____

5 _____

6 _____

7 _____

8 _____

9 _____

10 _____

Name: _____

Height: _____

Age: _____

Colour: _____

What Happened Today : _____

_____

_____

_____

_____

_____

_____

_____

_____

_____

Draw a Doodle!

I ♥ Horses

Name: _____

Height: _____

Age: _____

Colour: _____

What Happened Today : _____

_____

_____

_____

_____

_____

_____

_____

_____

_____

Stick a
A Pony Photo
HERE!

I ♥ Horses

Name: _____

Height: _____

Age: _____

Colour: _____

What Happened Today : _____

_____

_____

_____

_____

_____

_____

_____

_____

_____

Draw a Doodle!

I ♥ Horses

Colour me In

Name: _____

Height: _____

Age: _____

Colour: _____

What Happened Today : _____

_____

_____

_____

_____

_____

_____

_____

_____

_____

Draw a Doodle!

I ♥ Horses

Name: _____

Height: _____

Age: _____

Colour: _____

What Happened Today : _____

_____

_____

_____

_____

_____

_____

_____

_____

_____

Stick a
A Pony Photo
HERE!

I ♥ Horses

Can you name 10 horse movies?

1. _____

2. _____

3. _____

4. _____

5. _____

6. _____

7. _____

8. _____

9. _____

10. _____

Name: _____

Height: _____

Age: _____

Colour: _____

What Happened Today : _____

_____

_____

_____

_____

_____

_____

_____

_____

_____

Draw a Doodle!

I ♥ Horses

Story Time

The *Ugly* Pony

Angharad Thompson Rees

THE UGLY PONY

BONUS TALE FROM MAGICAL ADVENTURES & PONY TALES

ANGHARAD THOMPSON REES

THE UGLY PONY

"Her long mane and tail flowed, and somehow it looked like shimmering stars had become tangled within the ends."

STABLE TALK

She ruffled in the straw, all gangly legs and awkwardness. In fact, her matchstick legs were so long the poor beast could barely hoist herself up from the ground. She twisted and turned, and got herself into all sorts of knots and shapes, covering her mane and tail with strands of golden straw in the process. But she smiled because the world was new and exciting, and this was the very first time the foal had opened her eyes.

Her mother looked down at her new-born in the cool, dark stable, then suddenly, her long face twisted in curiosity and … something more. Something a little alarming. She looked at her foal with an expression that appeared to be … disgust.

"What, in Black Beauty's paddock, is that?" questioned the horse next door as she peered over the chest-height wall that divided their stables. And Mother Pony's cheeks turned red, but she said not a word.

"I can hardly believe she is the daughter of such prize-winning stock," said the retired mare in the stable on the other side. The old pony chomped on fresh meadow hay that filled the barn with a musky sweetness, in contrast to her bitter words.

"I—I don't understand," said Mother Pony after a few deep breaths. She craned her neck and head towards her baby to take a closer look. "She's so skinny and frail and pale-looking, and what's that awful lumpy-bump on her forehead?" With that, Mother Pony covered her new-born with more straw to stop the onlookers from leering.

The young foal's pale white eyelashes closed over her eyes, and she tried to go to sleep before anyone noticed her flowing tears and utter dismay.

GROWING PAINS

*M*any weeks and months went by and the young foal grew and altered in shape, much to the distaste of the other ponies at the prize-winning stud. You see, she was nothing like them. They were strong, compact, and powerful. The ponies competed all around the country, showing off their high-kneed trots and bowling canters in county shows and country fairs. Judges in bowler hats adorned the ponies with ribbons and rosettes and sashes to approve their beauty, and they wore them proudly upon their thick, muscular necks decorated with neat little plaits. For they were show ponies of the very finest sort. But the young foal they had nicknamed The Ugly Duckling (but we shall call her Bella), was not like any show pony they had ever seen.

"You are a disgrace to this stud yard!" cried a foal not much older than Bella. The foal trotted around the paddock with his perfect little tail held above his perfect little back. He was every inch a show pony. Bella slunk away as she always did whenever the show ponies tormented her, and hid under an old willow tree hoping its looming shadow would cover her from view.

"Ouch!" Bella said with a start, and looked upwards. She thought a branch must have fallen from the tree and landed on her head. Then she saw a red squirrel with beady black eyes staring back at her. He had a handful of acorns and a cheeky smile.

"Ouch!" Bella cried again, as the squirrel made a well-aimed hit with yet another acorn that smashed right at the centre of poor Bella's head. "What did you do that for?"

The squirrel smirked and his bushy tail twitched. "Well, you're a strange-looking thing. Not like any of the other ponies here. And what's that great big lump on your head?"

Bella shook her neck and mane, hoping her long forelock would cover up the undesirable lump on her forehead. All the other ponies had short, neat manes and forelocks, but not Bella. Her owners and stable staff kept Bella's tangled, colourless mane as long as possible to hide her ugly, bumpy head and scrawny neck.

"I don't know what the bump is, but it makes my mother embarrassed and makes the rest of the ponies laugh," said Bella with a lump in her throat.

"Oh! I don't think it's the bump on your head that does that," the squirrel began, and Bella felt a little hopeful. Perhaps, she considered, if there were another reason, she could work on it and try to fit in—and maybe then the other ponies would finally like her. "No, it's not *just* the bump that makes you look strange. For you also have long, gangly legs, and pale, pale skin, and a weird look in your eyes. I mean, why are they blue? It's just not right to be so different." And with another toss of an acorn and a twitch of his tail, the squirrel disappeared into the tree, leaving Bella feeling even more miserable than before.

BREAKING OUT

*A*nd thus, life continued in very much the same way for Bella. Winter passed, as did spring, and summer, and autumn, until it was winter again. Yet, nothing much changed for Bella until The Breaking Season.

The grooms at the show yard believed horses and ponies only come of age when they reach their fourth year—and that's when they get broken-in and taught how to behave like proper, perfect show ponies. Bella's fourth spring was fast approaching and young stock and older show ponies alike were ablaze with excitement and gossip.

"Who will be the best show pony?"

"Who will have the finest trot?"

"Who will be the first pony to win a rosette this show season?"

But perhaps, most cruelly of all, "How awful will The Ugly Duckling look under saddle?"

"I bet you'll be incredibly uncomfortable to ride," said one show pony whose training had already started.

"I'd say so too," said another with a smug look on his pretty little face. "Anyway, I've heard the owners will break you in just to get rid of you, so we won't have to look at your ugly face, or that horrid bump on your head that gets bigger by the day."

But Bella, with her pale coat that never really shone, watched on in silence and contemplation. She watched how the ponies did as they were told, and how they all paraded around, doing the same thing every day—all of them trying to be alike. It struck her as rather boring.

"Come on, Ugly Duckling," said a young man who always put the first bridle and saddle on each pony. "Let's be seeing what you're made of."

The man wasn't unkind; he didn't break ponies in the way the cowboys of old used to. There were no ropes tied to hooves or spurs dug into sides. The young man was gentle and took his time to explain to the ponies how they must behave with a rider upon their backs.

But Bella decided that she didn't want to be tamed. She didn't want a rider upon her back, and then … something in her wild heart stirred. She knew she didn't look like a show pony, and now she decided that she didn't want to be one either!

"Whoa, girl," called the young man, as Bella reared up on her thin legs and thrashed around. She darted this way and that while the groom tried to catch her. Mother Pony looked on with further embarrassment, while the elder show ponies tutted, and the younger ones laughed.

"You are a stain on this prize-winning stud yard," a pretty little pony neighed.

"Well then," Bella said with a snort and a stamp of her white, white hoof, "I shall leave!"

And she spun around and galloped as fast as her legs would take her towards the fence line that bordered the paddock. She covered much ground, her legs like flashes of lightning across the land, and hardly a sound followed her hooves. Her long mane and tail flowed, and somehow it looked like shimmering stars had become tangled within the ends. Her pale white coat glowed and glistened and shone under the pale springtime sun. And then, she jumped. She jumped over the fence line of the stud yard with grace and effortlessness, and on she galloped, her heart bursting with hope until she could see the stud yard no more.

A NEW DISCOVERY

*B*ella continued over sunlit hills and tree-covered valleys. She trotted through streams and cantered through rivers. She jumped over fallen logs and dry-stone wall fences. She galloped out every bad word anyone had ever said about her and for the first time in her life, Bella felt free.

She felt like… herself.

And most importantly, without the need to compare herself to the pretty, perfect show ponies that used to surround her; she no longer felt ugly. Out in the real world, she discovered, everyone and everything looked different. Everyone and everything *was* different. Where she had only before seen white sheep at the stud yard, now she saw black sheep and brown sheep, and sheep with cute tufts of wool on their heads. She saw cattle of every colour—some were even multi-coloured—and tall, or short, or fat. Trees were different shapes too; flowers grew in different crops with sweet, heady fragrances. Even the grass grew in several shades of green compared to the stud yard's one-tone grass.

"So," she said aloud just to hear the sound of a voice (she had no idea how long she had been travelling on her own. It may have been days, or months, or even years). "So, we're not all meant to look alike after all!"

And this idea soothed her as she entered a great wood; her snow-white hooves pressing softly into the forest loam of pine and leaves. Inside the wood, everything felt right, and she pondered if she was never meant for paddocks and show rings after all. Maybe, Bella considered, she was made for the forest. Perhaps that was why she always gravitated to the big old willow tree that stood in the middle of the stud yard.

Sun filtered between thick branches, offering gentle warmth in the cool canopy. Bella's pale-blue eyes took in every detail of what she decided would be her new home. And then she came across a squirrel and stopped in her tracks. So too, did the tail-twitching beast. This squirrel was a little different from the last creature she had met—he was grey and large and wide-eyed. Bella noticed the forest creature holding an acorn in his tiny, clawed fists, and prepared herself for the impact on her head. She also prepared herself for the horrible words and jibes, as this was the first time she had got close to another animal since her travels had begun.

The squirrel gasped.

She's probably never seen such an ugly beast, Bella thought sadly. And she lowered her head and neck in embarrassment.

"Come! Quick!" cried the squirrel, looking around the forest. He hopped on each leg in turn and called and called, and called out again. A bad moment got even worse for poor Bella as, within moments, hundreds of forest beasts surrounded the poor pony. She prepared herself for the onslaught of mockery and cruel, cruel, words. Birds and butterflies swooped onto branches. Hedgehogs and badgers waddled towards her hooves. Wild boars, swift deer, and an entire menagerie gathered close by. Bella's heart sank, and she felt the tears well in her pale-blue eyes. And then, worst of all, if it was even possible, she heard the gentle footfalls of another pony.

Bella felt as though she had been running away from her fears only to face them once again. But as the hoof beats became closer, and the pony came out from behind the trees, Bella gasped. The forest animals bowed their heads in respect.

Standing proud in front of Bella was the tallest, palest, and whitest pony she had *never* imagined seeing. The other pony stopped and stood tall—her eyes as pale as the water in the spring streams Bella had galloped through. Her legs were long and elegant and slender, her mane and tail flowed upon the ground and dazzled with stars and moonbeams (and something else spectacular that Bella couldn't put a name to). Perhaps, she thought, what she was seeing was magic. And there, placed right at the centre of the pony's forehead was a long, mesmerising single horn.

"You, you are beautiful!" Bella exclaimed. She could not

help herself and felt immediately foolish for saying so. But the beast smiled back and Bella felt like the world had turned in a different direction.

"And so are you," she said.

Bella shook her mane in confusion. "Me? Beautiful?" she wondered if this was a cruel joke.

She smiled, this pale, white magnificent beast. "Tell me, child, what is your name?" she asked.

"I'm Bella, but everyone always calls me The Ugly Duckling." Her pale cheeks flushed a little.

All the small creatures watched on in utter silence; only their eyes moved from one pony to the other as each spoke.

"Funny," said the older pony, "there was once a famous tale about an ugly duckling— and he was also nothing of the sort either. Bella of the Forest Path, you are no ugly duckling. You are a unicorn."

Now the forest creatures bowed in reverence.

"A unicorn? But I thought I was just a poorly bred, ugly show pony," Bella said, her ocean eyes swimming with hope.

"You were never a show pony and here is the secret— nobody is ever beautiful when they try to be something they are not. All you need to be beautiful, is to be yourself, Bella of The Forest Path."

Bella's heart swelled to hear those words, and as she reared up high; the animals around cheered.

"Here, come," said the magnificent beast, and Bella followed her to a clear white river flowing through the woods. "Take a look, for you do not need others to tell you that you are beautiful, you should know it for yourself."

And Bella did, seeing her true self, her true reflection in the clear waters, for the very first time. The ugly bump on her head had grown and morphed into a mesmerising single horn that glittered and shimmered. And she knew then that she should never compare herself to others, because she was perfect just the way she was.

Bella smiled at the other unicorn, the first pony to ever show her kindness, and asked,

"What is your name?"

She smiled. "I'm Faith of the Onward Journey."

"Thank you, Faith, for showing me who I truly am."

"You found it all by yourself simply by having the courage to follow your heart."

The unicorns smiled at each other, all magic and happiness. And the pair walked deeper into the heart of the forest —hidden away from the eyes of the show ponies and from the eyes of any who do not recognise their true beauty, which is the way of the unicorn and, perhaps, why they are quite so hard to find.

The End

Your Turn to Write a Horsey Story!

Story Title

_____

Written by

_____

Draw your Book Cover!

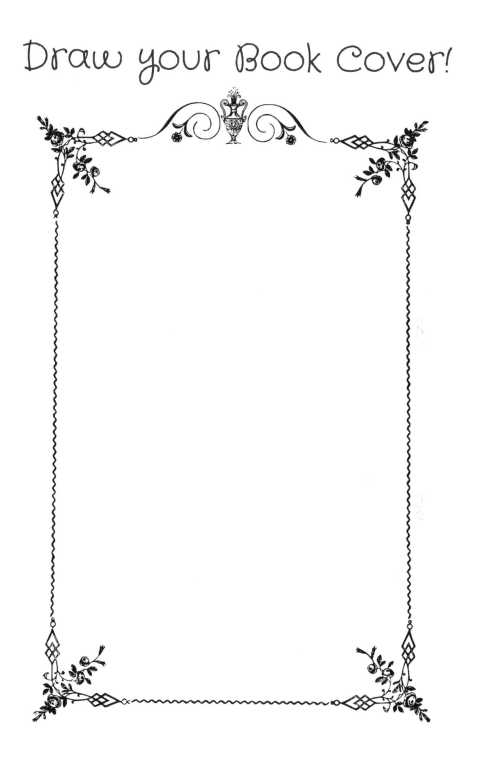

Once upon a time . . .

_____

_____

_____

_____

_____

_____

_____

_____

_____

_____

_____

_____

Awesome!
You wrote a story!

Let's see it!

Want to see your story or pony doodles on the author's Fan Page?

Send them in to:

hello@angharadthompsonrees.com

Can you name 10 famous horses?

1 _____

2 _____

3 _____

4 _____

5 _____

6 _____

7 _____

8 _____

9 _____

10 _____

Name: _____

Height: _____

Age: _____

Colour: _____

What Happened Today : _____

_____

_____

_____

_____

_____

_____

_____

_____

Stick a
A Pony Photo
HERE!

Name: _____

Height: _____

Age: _____

Colour: _____

What Happened Today : _____

_____

_____

_____

_____

_____

_____

_____

_____

_____

Draw a Doodle!

I ♥ Horses

Name: _____

Height: _____

Age: _____

Colour: _____

What Happened Today : _____

_____

_____

_____

_____

_____

_____

_____

_____

_____

Stick a
A Pony Photo
HERE!

CAN YOU NAME ALL THE PARTS OF THE SADDLE?

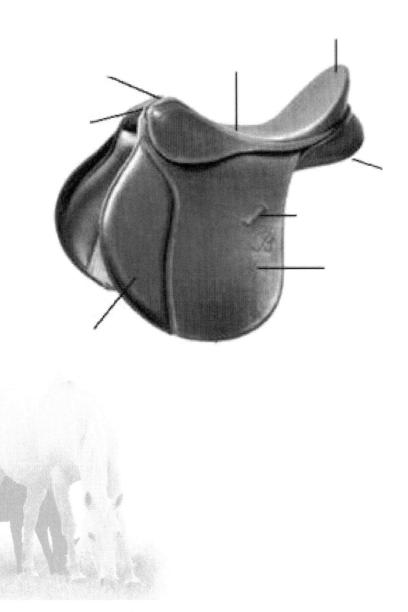

Can you name 10 horse sports?

1 _____

2 _____

3 _____

4 _____

5 _____

6 _____

7 _____

8 _____

9 _____

10 _____

Draw a Doodle!

I ♥ Horses

Name: _____

Height: _____

Age: _____

Colour: _____

What Happened Today : _____

_____

_____

_____

_____

_____

_____

_____

_____

Stick a
A Pony Photo
HERE!

Name: _____

Height: _____

Age: _____

Colour: _____

What Happened Today : _____

_____

_____

_____

_____

_____

_____

_____

_____

_____

Draw a Doodle!

I ♡ Horses

Pony Poems!

Can you write a poem in RHYMING COUPLETS?

What is a rhyming couplet, you ask?

A rhyming couplet has two lines, and the last word at the end of each line rhyme, like this...

A) I've never seen a flying **horse**
A) Because they don't exist of **course**

Add two more lines to get a full verse...

B) But if I found one I would **cry**
B) "Let us gallop through the **sky!"**

The A lines rhyme, and the B lines rhyme.
How many AABB verses can you do?
Can you make a full story in a poem?

Go on! Give it a go!

Pony Poem

Here's an example to get you inspired!

I've never seen a flying horse
because they don't exist, of course
But if I saw one I would cry
"Let us gallop through the sky!"

We'd canter to the blazing sun
laughing at the joy and fun
jumping clouds both high and low
and sliding down a big rainbow

Though when it's time for us to land
I won't be sad to understand
the secret that I'll have to keep
to meet this horse in my sleep

For people think they don't exist
no matter how much I persist
to tell them of my flying horse
who lives inside my dreams of course!

I ♥ Horses

Pony Poem # 1

I ♥ Horses

Pony Poem # 2

I ♥ Horses

Pony Poem # 3

I ♥ Horses

Pony Poem # 4

You're a poet
and you know it!

I ♥ Horses

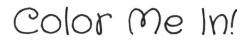

Color Me In!

I ♥ Horses

Name: _____

Height: _____

Age: _____

Colour: _____

What Happened Today : _____

_____

_____

_____

_____

_____

_____

_____

_____

_____

Pony Poem # 5

I ♥ Horses

Name: _____

Height: _____

Age: _____

Colour: _____

What Happened Today : _____

_____

_____

_____

_____

_____

_____

_____

_____

_____

Stick a
A Pony Photo
HERE!

I ♥ Horses

Name: _____

Height: _____

Age: _____

Colour: _____

What Happened Today : _____

_____

_____

_____

_____

_____

_____

_____

_____

_____

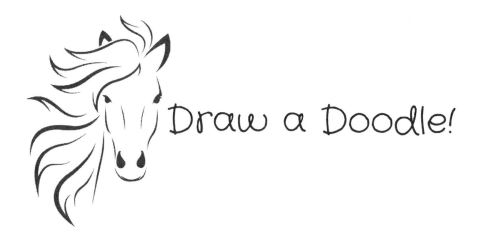

Draw a Doodle!

I ♥ Horses

Name: _____

Height: _____

Age: _____

Colour: _____

What Happened Today : _____

_____

_____

_____

_____

_____

_____

_____

_____

_____

Pony Poem # 6

I ♥ Horses

Name: _____

Height: _____

Age: _____

Colour: _____

What Happened Today : _____

_____

_____

_____

_____

_____

_____

_____

_____

_____

Stick a
A Pony Photo
HERE!

I ♥ Horses

Pony Poem # 7

I ♥ Horses

Name: _____

Height: _____

Age: _____

Colour: _____

What Happened Today : _____

_____

_____

_____

_____

_____

_____

_____

_____

_____

Draw a Doodle!

I ♥ Horses

Name: _____

Height: _____

Age: _____

Colour: _____

What Happened Today : _____

_____

_____

_____

_____

_____

_____

_____

_____

_____

Stick a
A Pony Photo
HERE!

Pony Poem # 8

I ♥ Horses

Pony Poem # 9

I ♥ Horses

Pony Poem # 10

Great work!

Can you name 10 famous Riders?

1 _____

2 _____

3 _____

4 _____

5 _____

6 _____

7 _____

8 _____

9 _____

10 _____

Name: _____

Height: _____

Age: _____

Colour: _____

What Happened Today : _____

_____

_____

_____

_____

_____

_____

_____

_____

Draw a Doodle!

I ♥ Horses

Name: _____

Height: _____

Age: _____

Colour: _____

What Happened Today : _____

_____

_____

_____

_____

_____

_____

_____

_____

_____

Stick a
A Pony Photo
HERE!

I ♥ Horses

Name: _____

Height: _____

Age: _____

Colour: _____

What Happened Today : _____

_____

_____

_____

_____

_____

_____

_____

_____

_____

Draw a Doodle!

I ♥ Horses

Name: _____

Height: _____

Age: _____

Colour: _____

What Happened Today : _____

_____

_____

_____

_____

_____

_____

_____

_____

_____

Stick a
A Pony Photo
HERE!

I ♥ Horses

Can you name 10 Olympic horses?

1 _____

2 _____

3 _____

4 _____

5 _____

6 _____

7 _____

8 _____

9 _____

10 _____

Name: _____

Height: _____

Age: _____

Colour: _____

What Happened Today : _____

_____

_____

_____

_____

_____

_____

_____

_____

 Draw a Doodle!

 I ♥ Horses

Name: _____

Height: _____

Age: _____

Colour: _____

What Happened Today : _____

_____

_____

_____

_____

_____

_____

_____

_____

_____

Draw a Doodle!

I ♥ Horses

Name: _____

Height: _____

Age: _____

Colour: _____

What Happened Today : _____

_____

_____

_____

_____

_____

_____

_____

_____

Stick a
A Pony Photo
HERE!

I ♥ Horses

Well Done!

You've completed your
Horse Riding Journal!

1st Place

About the Author

Angharad Thompson Rees is the author of the Magical Adventures and Pony Tales series, and comic scriptwriter for a popular pony magazine.

She has spent her lifetime frolicking with horses and ponies, from Olympic show jumpers and world class racehorses, to taming naughty ponies using Horse Whispering techniques.

She believes in the magical, revels in the whimsical and owns a pet unicorn, called Sydney.

You can find out more at:

www.angharadthompsonrees.com

Magical Adventures & Pony Tales

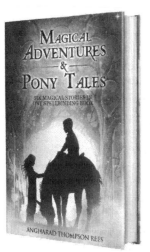

*****

"This is a fabulous collection of magical horse stories that horse crazy children will adore"

*****

"If you love ponies, these stories are just right for you. They are all filled with love and magic."

*****

"A fantastic collection of heartwarming pony tales perfect for any young (or old) horse lover. The perfect length for bedtime stories, and imaginative dreams. I would recommend this book to anyone."

Made in the USA
San Bernardino, CA
16 December 2019